Creatures in Danger
Alison Hawes

Contents

Ruth's Journal

Ruth Trotter
Aged 10

6th August
I love surprises and today I had two! First, Mum told me Uncle Globe would be joining us on holiday (yay!) and second, a parcel arrived all the way from America with my name on it! I was meant to be packing for our holiday when it arrived (we're off camping tomorrow — same place as last year) but I couldn't wait to open it!

Uncle 'Globe' Trotter

My brothers Zac and Joel

ME! (Ruth)

Our cousin Reema

Rock-pooling in Dorset, on the South Coast.

Here we all are on holiday last year when Uncle Globe took us rock-pooling. His real name is Jim Trotter but Zac started calling him Globe as a joke and now everyone calls him that! Globe is a famous explorer and a conservationist.

POST

This letter was inside my parcel.

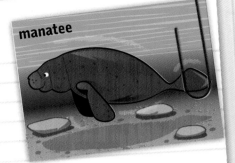

manatee

Florida
USA
3rd August

Hi Ruth,
I've been having the most amazing time over here, helping to conserve these gentle giants — but now it's time for me to head back to the UK to help out on another marine conservation project and join you all on holiday. So I thought I'd set you a little challenge to keep you busy until I arrive!
The first part of my challenge is for you to work out which marine creature I am going to help conserve in the UK. The book I've sent you should help you work out the answer and I've also added a scrapbook for you to keep your answers and ideas in.
There will be more questions along the way but if you are successful, I have a great day out in mind for you as a reward.
So good luck! Let me know how you get on.

Globe

I think this means he's going to help keep some creatures from harm.

My first challenge!

Well, I can't resist a challenge, so I forgot the packing and opened the book straight away ...

3

The Coastline

Small country, big coast

For a small country, the UK has an incredibly long coastline. This is because the UK is made up of *over 1000 islands* which all add up to a whopping 11 000 miles of coastline!

The UK coast and the seas that surround it are home to an amazing **array** of wildlife, from huge sharks to tiny worms!

Now you see it, now you don't!

The coastline is constantly changing. Over time cliffs and rocks wear away and change shape, as they are **eroded** by the sea. At the same time, beaches and land appear and disappear, as the sea **deposits** the rock and soil it has worn away, in different places.

What to spot!

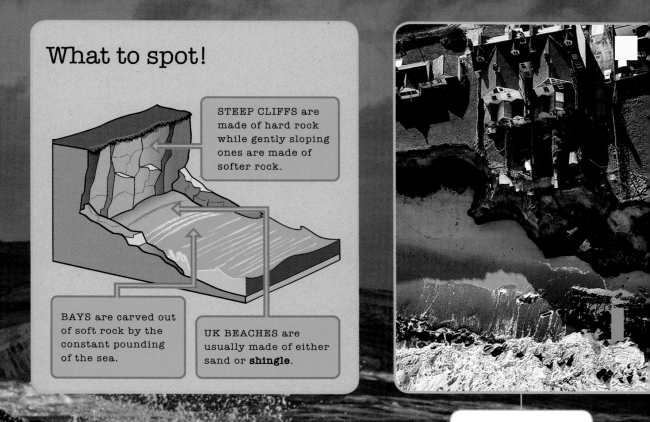

STEEP CLIFFS are made of hard rock while gently sloping ones are made of softer rock.

BAYS are carved out of soft rock by the constant pounding of the sea.

UK BEACHES are usually made of either sand or **shingle**.

The erosion of soft cliffs can cause landslides!

Did you know?

Over 25 million holidays and 200 million day trips are taken around the UK coast each year.

The creature you are looking for can be found in the sea near where we are going camping. What sea is that?
Globe

Creatures on the Edge

The sandy shore

Sometimes a beach can look strangely empty, but take a closer look and you may find small marine creatures hidden under the wet sand. Look out for small spirals of sand on the surface as these often indicate where creatures may be hiding.

otter

Dunes

Sand

Beach creatures

If you are lucky, you may spot a much bigger animal like a seal or an otter on a beach. The otters that live by the sea in the UK are the same as river otters but they have adapted to life on the coast.

Beach

Conger eels have smooth, scaleless skin.

Hidden in the shallows

Many other creatures have adapted to life amongst the sand, rocks and grasses out in the shallow water beyond the low tide mark. Conger eels can be found hidden amongst rocks. They can grow up to 2.75 m long!

On the rocks

Small animals, like hairy crabs, can be found in rock pools at low tide.
A hairy crab is easy to spot: one of its claws is bigger than the other,
and its shell and legs are hairy, of course!

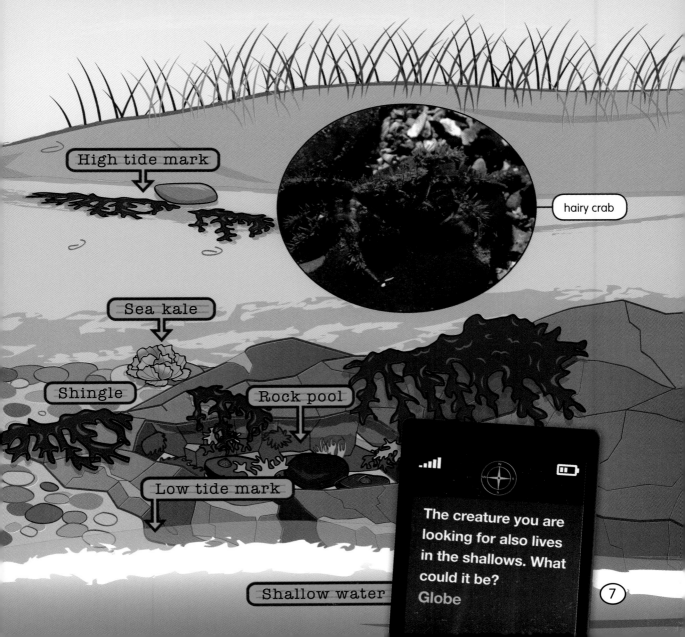

High tide mark

hairy crab

Sea kale

Shingle

Rock pool

Low tide mark

The creature you are looking for also lives in the shallows. What could it be?
Globe

Shallow water

Creatures out at Sea

Weird and wonderful

Even more fantastic marine creatures make their home further out to sea. Some swim near the top of the water where it is light and warm. Others have adapted to living near or on the deep seabed where it is cold and dark. These are the creatures you rarely get to see.

Big mouth

The largest fish in UK waters is the basking shark. It often swims close to the surface with part of its snout and fins showing above the surface. This enormous fish, with its huge open mouth, looks fierce, but is in fact quite harmless to humans and fish.

Shoal of mackerel

Smooth scales

Mackerel swim in great shoals or schools in the open sea. In summer they move closer to the shore to feed on the small fish and prawns found there. Mackerel do have scales but they are so small their skin feels velvety to touch!

> Wolf fish even have teeth in their throat!

Fangs

Wolf fish can be found up to 500m down in the sea. They have fang-like teeth at the front of their mouth and big teeth at the back, for crushing their prey. With teeth like that, they have no problems snapping up crabs and clams or any other creatures with a hard shell.

Did you know?

A basking shark sifts two Olympic sized swimming pools' worth of seawater through its mouth and gills every day, to trap the **plankton** it feeds on.

Basking shark

The creature you are looking for is small and eats plankton. What could it be?

Globe

Unexpected Creatures

The seas around the UK are also home to some surprising and unexpected creatures.

Ultimate predator

Killer whales or orca are part of the dolphin family. They live in every ocean and sea in the world, including the seas around the UK. At times, groups of up to one hundred orca have been spotted.

Killer whales often hunt in shallow water.

Seahorses

When we think of seahorses we often think of brightly coloured coral reefs, but these shy creatures live in the UK's waters all year round. They are found in shallow water close to the seabed.

Seahorses eat very small marine animals, like tiny shrimp and plankton.

Bright colours

Brightly coloured fish are usually **associated** with warm tropical seas but, believe it or not, this gurnard with its bright red body is found in the UK's cold seas.

The gurnard has **iridescent** fins.

Sea squirt

This most surprising creature is a light-bulb sea squirt. Sea squirts are small, sometimes **transparent**, jelly-like animals, which attach themselves to rocks and shells under the sea.

This light-bulb sea squirt was found off the coast of Wales.

Think:

How did the light-bulb sea squirt get its name?

Have you worked out which creature it is yet? Think about what you know so far. Need one last clue? The creature is a very unusual-looking fish!

Globe

Fishy Business

6th August

After reading some of the book Globe sent me, I was sure that he was going to help protect seahorses.

Zac said it couldn't possibly be a seahorse, as a seahorse isn't a fish because it doesn't have scales.

But I said it is a fish as it has fins.

Anyway, I texted Globe and he said I was right! He is going to work on a seahorse conservation project.

So it's Ruth: One – Zac: Nil!

Then he sent me this email with the next part of the challenge.

Ruth

From: Globetrotter
To: Ruth Trotter
Sent: 6th August 16:22
Subject: Challenge

Hi Ruth,

Well done for working out the animal was a seahorse.

Now for the next part of your challenge: I need you to find out all you can about seahorses and where they can be found in the UK.

I've attached a chart for you to fill in that should help you discover the sorts of place seahorses can be found in the UK. (This will be useful when it's time to claim your reward!)

Good luck.

Globe

P.S. Don't forget to pack your wetsuit – you are going to need it!

Where you find seahorses you will also find:	Sometimes	Always
Shrimp and plankton		
Sea grass		
Shallow water		
Rock pools		
Algae		

So, on the long drive to the campsite, I opened Globe's book at the section on seahorses ...

Surprising Seahorses

Funny fish

Seahorses *are* fish, even
though they are neither
fish-shaped nor covered
in scales. But like most
fish they have:

- gills to help them breathe
- fins to help them move
- a swim bladder to help
  them float or sink.

Dad gives birth

The female seahorse lays her eggs
in a pouch on the front of the male.
The male fertilises the eggs in his
pouch and the pouch expands and
becomes more rounded as the baby
seahorses grow inside. Then in two
to four weeks the male gives birth to
lots of **miniature** seahorses or fry.

   It is the only animal in the world where
the dad truly gives birth! But neither the
mum nor the dad feeds or takes care of
their young after the birth. The fry must
search for their own food and look after
themselves from the second they are born.

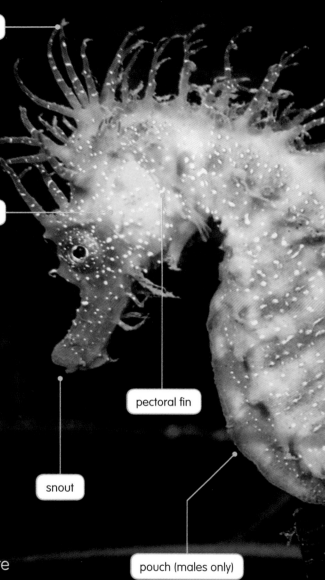

coronet

gills

pectoral fin

snout

pouch (males only)

Seahorse facts

- Seahorses have no true stomach, so they have to eat almost continuously – just to stay alive!
- Seahorses have no teeth. They feed by hoovering up plankton and shrimp, through their snout. They suck the food in with such force that it gets broken up into tiny pieces before they swallow it.
- A seahorse's eyes move **independently** of one another, so they can look backwards and forwards for food (and predators) at the same time!

bony ridges

dorsal fin

Plankton consists of **microscopic** plants and animals that float in the sea. There are two kinds of plankton, **zooplankton** and **phytoplankton**.

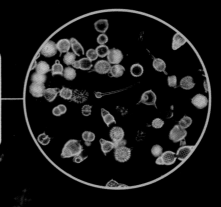

Think:

Which of these words means animal plankton and which one means plant plankton?

tail

Why do you think living close to a constant source of food is important to a seahorse?
Globe

Seahorses in the UK

Different species

There have been seahorses in the world for at least 40 million years! There are now over thirty different **species** of seahorse but only two species are found along the UK coast: the spiny and the short snouted seahorse.

The spiny seahorse can live for up to 7 years!

Spiny

A spiny seahorse can grow up to 18 cm long and, as its name suggests, it often has long spines on its body.

It also has a slightly longer snout than the short snouted seahorse, which is why it is sometimes called the long snouted seahorse.

Fin facts

- Because they are not fish-shaped, seahorses are poor swimmers.
- A fin on their back helps them to move through the water.
- Little fins either side of their head help them to balance and steer.

Short snout

Short snouted seahorses rarely grow spines and tend to be a little shorter than spiny seahorses, growing up to 17 cm long.

Tail talk

All seahorses have a **prehensile** tail which they wrap around seaweed or sea grass, or each other, to stop themselves being washed away by strong currents or waves.

Short snouted seahorses are less common than spiny seahorses.

Did you know?

The fin on a seahorse's back can beat up to 70 times a second!

Why do you think seahorses are sometimes found living amongst sea grasses and algae?
Globe

17

Home Sweet Home

Different habitats

UK seahorses make their homes in different places. Sometimes they can be found amongst sea grass or algae. Sometimes they can be found in rock pools or sandy **estuaries.**

Pipefish

What to look for

Some of the other marine creatures that often share a seahorse's habitat are:

- *Pipefish* which are relatives of the seahorse.
- *Cuttlefish* which are from the same family as octopuses.
- *Flatfish* which can camouflage themselves well in the seabed.

Cuttlefish

Underwater meadow

The spiny seahorse seems to prefer living amongst sea grass or algae-covered rocks where it can stay hidden.

Flatfish

Sea grass or eel grass is a grass-like flowering plant. It grows in shallow sheltered areas of the UK's seas such as bays and estuaries.

Where to look

Seahorses have been found from Scotland in the north, down the West Coast of the UK, to the English Channel in the south and all around Ireland.

In particular, important **colonies** of seahorses have been found off the Devon and Dorset coasts.

Seahorses found around the UK

Short snouted seahorse

Spiny seahorse

ATLANTIC OCEAN

NORTH SEA

IRISH SEA

ENGLISH CHANNEL

N
W E
S

Short snouted seahorses tend to be found in a wider variety of habitats than the spiny seahorse and have even been found in areas of open sand or silt.

One of the most important sites in the UK – if not the world! – for spiny seahorses is Studland Bay, in Dorset on the South Coast.

Look back at the chart I gave you. What things do we need to look for to find where seahorses live?

Globe

By the Sea

7th August

We arrived here this afternoon. The campsite is great and I've got my own tent for once, so no more sharing with my noisy brothers! We're only a few miles from the coast, so the wetsuit Globe told me to pack will come in useful.

I was amazed by some of the facts I learned about seahorses today:

Head like a horse?

Eyes like a chameleon?

Pouch like a kangaroo?

Tail like a monkey?

It must be a seahorse!

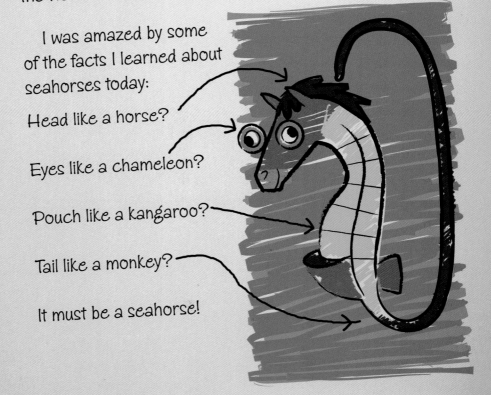

I was pleased to find that both kinds of seahorse are found all along the South Coast, so I'm wondering if I might even see some on holiday!

I texted Globe on Zac's mobile to let him know that I had filled in his chart.

Where you find seahorses you will also find:	Sometimes	Always
Shrimp and plankton		✓
Sea grass	✓	
Shallow water		✓
Rock pools	✓	
Algae	✓	

Here's what Globe texted back:

Great work Ruth :-)

Now for the final part of your challenge.

See if you can find out what people are doing to protect seahorses in the UK.

This will be useful to know on your reward day out! No need to text back. I should be at the campsite in time for breakfast!

Globe x

It was getting dark by then, so I snuggled down in my tent and read more of Globe's book by torchlight ...

Seahorses in Danger

For sale

Every year, across the world, millions of seahorses are hunted and sold:

- as pets
- as souvenirs
- for use in traditional Chinese medicines.

In some countries, seahorses are taken from the sea and left to dry out in the hot sun before being sold to tourists.

Predators

Because seahorses have bony plates covered in skin to protect their bodies, instead of scales, many larger fish and marine animals don't find seahorses good to eat. However, in the UK, fish like bass or mackerel and seagulls will make a meal of seahorses – if they can find them! By changing the colour of their skin to match their surroundings, seahorses find it easy to disappear.

Destruction

Sea grass meadows are an important home for seahorses, young fish and shellfish but, bit by bit, some of these meadows are being destroyed.

Damage to a sea grass bed by an anchor.

Causes

The main causes of the destruction are:

1. fishing boats working in shallow waters that sometimes pull up the sea grass as they fish
2. boat owners who destroy the sea grass by dumping rubbish or anchoring their boats amongst the grass.

What do you think could be done to protect the sea grass meadows around the UK's shores?
Globe

Conservation Work

Census

Since 1994, the British Seahorse Survey has been working to find out how many seahorses live around the UK's coast and where. They rely on help from the public to do this. So if you ever spot a seahorse, do not touch it, but make a note of where you saw it and let The Seahorse Trust know. Results from the survey show that seahorses don't always live in sea grass meadows (as had previously been thought). Recording where seahorses have been seen has allowed The Seahorse Trust to map where they live.

Conservationists like The Seahorse Trust are working hard in the UK to find out more about seahorses and to protect them and their habitats.

Tagging

Conservationists from The Seahorse Trust are beginning to tag seahorses in Studland Bay, Dorset, to help them learn more about the lives of these shy creatures and how best to conserve them.

Each little plastic tag is on a thin piece of elastic and has a number on it to identify each seahorse.

Measuring

As well as tagging, conservationists in Dorset are measuring and photographing local seahorses and recording their location. They use **GPS** to log a seahorse's location so they can find them again more easily.

Conservationists need a special licence to handle seahorses.

Knowledge

The work of conservationists in seas and aquariums has meant that more is now known about seahorses and other marine life than ever before, and about the importance of protecting them.

What should you do if you see a seahorse? Globe

Making a Difference

Against the law

Due to pressure from The Seahorse Trust, there is now a law in the UK that makes it **illegal** for someone to deliberately harm seahorses or their habitat.

Sightings of seahorses are slowly increasing. This conservationist has found a pregnant seahorse.

The waters around the island of Skomer in Wales form one of the three Marine Nature Reserves that have been set up around the UK so far.

Protected

Conservationists are also keen to set up special areas around the UK's coast where marine life will be protected, such as marine nature reserves and **No Take Zones**. But despite this, many areas where seahorses live are still not yet fully protected.

Think:
What is meant by a No Take Zone?

Education

Because people and marine animals often share the same places, conservation groups are working to find ways to help visitors to the UK's coasts enjoy their visit, *without* harming the wildlife or themselves. Asking people to follow the Seashore Code is just one idea.

Seashore Code

Always keep an eye on the tide.
Walk carefully over rocks.

Take your litter home.

Take home photos, not plants and animals.
Do not anchor your boats in sea grass meadows.

**Keep away from the cliff edge.
Treat all wildlife with respect.
Our coast is there to enjoy.
Not to destroy!**

What more do you think could be done to protect seahorses and other marine life? Globe

Rewarded

9th August

Globe arrived in time for breakfast, yesterday, just as he said he would. We were all so pleased to see him that we all talked at once! But later on, Globe spoke to me about his challenge and all the things I had learned. I told him about the conservation work that was already being done around our coasts, to count the seahorses and to protect their habitats.

Globe said if seahorses are to be properly protected, there need to be even more protected areas around our coast and a ban on boat owners anchoring in sea grass meadows.

Breakfast at our campsite

11th August

Today, I got my reward! Globe went diving off the Dorset coast with a group of conservationists who were photographing and measuring the seahorses they found – and I was allowed to go along and help!

As Globe is a conservationist, he has a special licence to handle seahorses. His job was to carefully hold the seahorses while their photos were taken with an underwater camera. At first, it was difficult to spot any seahorses. They were so well camouflaged! Finally, we saw two juveniles and an adult.

Then as we were about to go back up to the surface, I spotted a pregnant seahorse. I kept very still so I didn't disturb it and called Globe over.

Everyone was very pleased with me because it was the only pregnant seahorse to be found there for some time!

When I got back to school after the summer holidays, I was interviewed by the school newspaper for their September edition.

Save our

Ruth Trotter tells our School News reporter about her unusual find.

Year 5 student, Ruth Trotter, was having fun on a family camping holiday in Dorset last month when her uncle, well-known explorer and conservationist Mr Jim 'Globe' Trotter, took her for a surprise day out, diving in the beautiful Studland Bay.

But this was no ordinary dive. Globe was working with The Seahorse Trust helping to photograph and measure the seahorses in the bay and Ruth was given the very rare opportunity to help out. Ruth was able to see at first hand the important work these conservationists are doing and was doubly thrilled to be the only one on the day to spot a pregnant male!

Seahorses

That's right – in the seahorse world, it is the male not the female that gives birth to up to 300 fry at a time! Ruth said, "Unfortunately most seahorse fry are eaten by predators soon after they are born and those that do survive urgently need our help." She explained that the sea grass meadows found off the UK coasts are an important habitat for many of our seahorses, but that they are being destroyed by the thoughtless actions of some boat owners. "What is needed," Ruth suggested, "is a ban on anchoring boats in these areas or another way of mooring the boats that doesn't pull up the sea grass."

Note from the editor: Want to find out more about seahorses? Why not check out the website of The Seahorse Trust?

The Seahorse Trust

Glossary

algae simple plants without roots, stems or leaves, living mainly in water

array wide selection

associated connected

colony large group

deposits leaves, places something

eroded worn away

estuary where the river meets the sea

GPS Global Positioning System, a network of satellites that allows users to track their location very accurately

illegal against the law

independently on their own

iridescent shiny, rainbow coloured

microscopic so small it can only be seen with a microscope

miniature very small

No Take Zone an area from which no marine creature may be taken

phytoplankton plant plankton

plankton microscopic sea plants and animals

prehensile able to grasp, hold on

shingle pebbles

species kind or sort

transparent see-through

zooplankton animal plankton

Index